Alfred Sandham

McGill College and its medals

Alfred Sandham

McGill College and its medals

ISBN/EAN: 9783742865175

Manufactured in Europe, USA, Canada, Australia, Japa

Cover: Foto ©Paul-Georg Meister /pixelio.de

Manufactured and distributed by brebook publishing software
(www.brebook.com)

Alfred Sandham

McGill College and its medals

JAMES McGILL

McGILL COLLEGE

McGill College

AND ITS

MEDALS

BY

Alfred Sandham,

AUTHOR OF "COINS OF CANADA," "MONTREAL PAST AND PRESENT," "PRINCE OF
WALES MEDALS." CORRESPONDING MEMBER OF THE AMER. NUM. AND ARCH. SOC.
(N. YORK), NUMISMATIC SOCIETIES OF BOSTON AND PHILADELPHIA, AND
THE NEW ENGLAND HISTORIC-GENEALOGICAL SOC. (BOSTON).

ILLUSTRATED BY W. NOTMAN,

PHOTOGRAPHER TO THE QUEEN.

Montreal:

D. BENTLEY & CO., PRINTERS, 364 NOTRE DAME STREET.

1872.

DEDICATED

TO

J. W. DAWSON, LL.D., F.R.S., F.G.S.

Principal and Vice-Chancellor

OF

McGILL UNIVERSITY.

PREFACE.

The object contemplated by this work is twofold in its nature, namely :—to furnish the friends of McGill College with a reliable account of its origin and subsequent progress ; and to supply additional information upon the subject of Canadian Numismatics. I have, therefore, employed the utmost care, and directed an unremitting attention, to comprehend what is most important and interesting in the subject before me. To attain this end, I have had recourse to " Articles on the Colleges of Canada," by Hon. P. J. O. Cheauveau ; " Biographical Sketch of Mr. McGill," with other works by Principal Dawson ; the Reports of the Governors ; and the records of the College.

With these advantages, I have endeavored to seize on the general outline of the history, and to fill it up with the most material subordinate notices selected from these sources, and I desire to acknowledge, that in many instances, instead of assuming originality by clothing the thoughts and opinions of others in my own expression, I prefer employing their own language, and I therefore resign to them the approbation due to their talents, desiring no further credit than such as may be thought due to my exertions in collecting and arranging the material for the work.

ALF. SANDHAM.

INTRODUCTION.

"Learning by study must be won ;
'Twas ne'er entailed from sire to son."—*Gay.*

The developement of the faculties, or germs of power in man, and the training of them into harmonious action in obedience to the laws of reason and morality, is what is comprehended in the term education. Yet education not only aims at the developement and culture of the child as an individual, but is also the means by which every rising generation is put in possession of all the attainments of preceding generations. In the earliest ages, the entire education and culture of the people were in the hands of priests, who were the first founders of institutions, the first statesmen, judges, physicians and astronomers, and it is only in the most highly civilized communities that science has been separated from religion, and teaching made a distinct profession. Even in these, learning and schools are often to a greater or less extent, more or less directly, under the patronage and care of religious bodies, since religion has been esteemed by all nations the highest interest of society.

On the antiquity of schools it is not necessary to dilate. We read in Sacred Writ of a "School of Prophets" under the supervision of the prophet Samuel. Passing to later dates, we learn that the early culture of the Egyptians was such that the Greeks derived from them their first lessons in science and philosophy, and from them the Israelites obtained the knowledge which enabled them to measure and "divide the land." The inscriptions on their monuments also prove an early knowledge of geometry, astronomy, mensuration and surveying in Egypt.

It is impossible to fix the period when universities, in the modern acceptation of the term, were first established. When Charlemagne ascended the throne of France, we are told that no means of education existed in his dominions; and, in order to restore in some degree the spirit of letters, he invited strangers from other countries where learning was not so thoroughly extinguished. With the help of these he established schools in different cities of his empire; and all the power and influence of the court were employed in forwarding his endeavors.

By degrees the light of science began to shine more brightly; and teachers, whose genius enabled them to rise above their fellows, and to overstep the narrow bounds to which they had been restricted, arose in various places, and their lectures were attended by crowds of admiring listeners. The success of one teacher invited others to the same field, and the large number of scholars who frequented the school of an admired expounder of some new or favorite question, afforded ample room for the exertion of his talent and ingenuity.

It was in this manner that particular schools obtained a permanent celebrity, and that those associations of teachers were formed which were afterwards recognized by the civil and ecclesiastical power, and ultimately dignified with the name of "Universities." The oldest of the European universities, (said to have been founded by Charlemagne,) was that of Paris, whose form and constitution were in a great measure adopted by the founders of the two great English universities, Oxford and Cambridge, which till within the last half century were the only universities in England.

At a very early date in the history of America, the colonists directed attention to the importance of education. Six years after the first settlement had been made in the New England States, the following entry appears in their records, under date of October 28th, 1636; "the court agreed to give 400l. toward a schoale or colledge, whereof 200l. to bee paid the next yeare, and 200l. when the work is finished." Such is the origin of Harvard college, the oldest and most amply endowed educational institution of the United States. Four years prior to this date, the Jesuit Fathers had opened at Quebec a school, which has since become a flourishing college, and in 1657 the seminary of St. Sulpice was founded at Montreal. Twenty-seven years after the conquest of Canada (1787), Lord Dorchester, governor of the old province of Quebec, appointed a commission to enquire into the subject of education, but no action of importance was taken until 1802, when the "Royal Institution for the advancement of learning" was legally incorporated. Among the many who took a lively interest in the measures taken by the government towards the formation of this board was Mr. James McGill, who has handed down his name to posterity as the founder of the noble institution, a brief history of which will be given in this work.

McGill College and its Medals.

James McGill was born in Glasgow, Scotland, on the 6th of October, 1744, and received his early training and education in that country. Like many of his countrymen, he emigrated, when a young man to the new world, in search of fortune. He settled in Montreal and engaged successfully in mercantile pursuits. On the 2nd of December, 1776, he married Charlotte Guillemin, (daughter of the late Guillaume Guillemin, in his lifetime councillor of the King of France in Canada, lieutenant-general of the admiralty of Quebec, and judge of the court of prerogatives,) widow of the late François Amable Trottier Des Rivières.

Mr. McGill's long residence in Montreal, his integrity, public spirit and practical good sense, gained for him the confidence of his fellow-citizens, and he was elected their representative in parliament. He was subsequently appointed a member of the legislative and executive councils, and during the war of 1812 acted as a colonel and brigadier-general of militia.

Mr. McGill is described by his contemporaries as a man of tall and commanding figure—in his youth a very handsome man, but becoming corpulent in his old age. He was a prominent member of the association of fur magnates known as the "Beaver Club." A reminiscence of a gentlemen, then resident in Montreal, represents him, when a very old man, at one of the meetings singing a *voyageur's* song with accurate ear and sonorous voice, and imitating, paddle in hand, the action of the bow-man of a "North canoe" in ascending a rapid. But though taking his full share in the somewhat jovial social life of that early time, Mr. McGill was always esteemed a temperate man, and was distinguished for his charity, his sound judgment, and his kindness of heart. The remembrance of another contemporary represents him as much given to reading and full of varied information; and it is certain that he cultivated and enjoyed the society of the few men of learning from the mother country then in the colony. He died in Montreal, on the 19th December, 1813, at the age of sixty-nine years.

Not having any children, he had determined to devote a large portion of his fortune to some object of benevolence connected with his adopted country; and in his last will, made two years before his decease, he set apart his beautifully situated estate of Burnside, on the slope of the Montreal mountain, with a sum of £10,000, for the foundation of a university, one of the colleges of which was to be named the McGill college. In this connection it may be stated that Mr. McGill's resolution to dispose of his property in this way was not a hasty death-bed resolve, but a mature and deliberate decision. He had taken a lively interest in the measures then before the Government for the establishment of an educational system in the province of Quebec, and had mentioned, many years before his death, his intention to give, during his lifetime, a sum of twenty thousand dollars in aid of a college, if these measures should be carried out by the Government. But many delays occurred. Unfortunately the relatives of Mr. McGill's widow were induced to dispute the validity of the will, and a protracted litigation ensued, which was not terminated till 1835; though in 1829 the landed property had been surrendered, and in the same year the college was formally organized under a Royal charter which had been obtained in 1821 in anticipation of the issue of the dispute respecting the endowment. The management of the endowment was to be confided to the " Royal Institution for the advancement of learning," and the bequest was to take effect on condition that there should be erected, within ten years, on the estate of Burnside, " a university or college for the purposes of education and the advancement of learning in this province, with a competent number of professors and teachers to render such establishment effectual and useful for the purposes intended."

Under the charter, the governor of Lower Canada, the lieutenant-governor of Upper Canada, the bishop of Quebec, the chief justice of Montreal, the chief justice of Upper Canada, and the principal, were ex-officio governors of the college, and were to elect its officers, and in conjunction with the fellows to constitute the corporation of the University, for the framing of its statutes and general management of its affairs. The Royal Institution was to retain a visitorial authority.

The college entered on its existence with much apparent vigor and promise of success. The opening ceremony was held in Burnside House, the former residence of the founder, and was largely attended. The first step toward the establishment of a University, was the organization in 1829 of the Faculty of Arts and the Medical Faculty. The former met with many difficulties and made little progress; but on the day of the inauguration the latter was accomplished by the union with it of the Montreal Medical Institute, which had already four professors, and an established reputation.

In 1835 Dr. Mountain, Principal of the University, resigned, and was succeeded by Rev. Dr. Bethune. In 1839 the erection of suitable buildings was commenced, and on 7th September, 1843, they were formally opened. In the erection of these buildings the governors had found it necessary to expend a large portion of the available means of the University, an outlay which the founder had never calculated upon, as he had given his endowment under the expectation that in accordance with the provisions of the act, large grants of land would have been placed at the disposal of the Royal Institution to supplement his bequest, as well as to provide for the general interests of education. This, however, the legislature failed to do, and the governors were unable at that early period to obtain from the landed property any considerable amount of income. The charter also had many defects, and was altogether too cumbrous. These with other disadvantages long rendered the efforts of the board of little avail, and for many years the University lingered on with little real growth. This languishing condition was a subject of deep regret and uneasiness to the friends of education in Montreal, but there appeared to be no practicable means of elevating it under the existing charter, and with its want of a sufficient revenue.

At length, in 1850, a number of gentlemen determined to grapple with these difficulties, and entered so heartily upon the work, that in 1852 an amended charter was secured, under which the managers began the labors of their trust. All useless expenses

were at once stopped. The only salary continued was one of a small amount to the vice-principal, which was necessary in order to prevent the college doors from being closed. An act was obtained empowering them to sell portions of the real estate bequeathed by Mr. McGill for a perpetual ground rent, with permission to mortgage the college property in security for a loan to the amount of £3,000. Under this law, sales were effected of a sufficient extent of the college lands to yield, when added to the former income, a revenue of £900. Application was also made to the legislature for pecuniary aid, and the sum of £1,300 was granted. In this way they were enabled to make arrangements for avoiding immediate pressure, and an opportunity was given to begin the work of providing an efficient and liberal course of instruction.

In 1853 the High school of Montreal was incorporated with McGill college, and became a distinct department of that institution. In the year 1854 an urgent appeal was made to the provincial government for liberal pecuniary assistance. The result was partially successful, but the sums received were very much less than those specified in the petition.

In 1846 Dr. Bethune resigned the principalship, and was succeeded by E. A. Meredith, Esq., who likewise resigned in 1853, when the Hon. C. D. Day, LL.D., was appointed under the new charter. He resigned in 1855, and Dr. Dawson was elected to the position which he still retains.

In consequence of the want of substantial support from the government, the governors determined to obtain assistance from other sources. An appeal was consequently made in December of the year 1856, to the Protestant population of Montreal, and was met as such appeals always have been by its leading citizens, in a spirit of unrestrained generosity. An endowment fund of £15,000 was subscribed, of which sum £5,000 were given by the Messrs. Molson, for founding a chair of English Literature.

In 1858 the legislature was again appealed to for aid, but without result, and although more than one of the gentlemen who then formed the Provincial Administration, rendered valuable aid, nevertheless, the paramount object of a permanent public endowment was not accomplished.

The inconvenience and difficulty arising from the want of room for carrying on the business of the University was not unfrequently a subject of conversation among the Governors, and regrets were often expressed that no means were available for adding to the College Buildings. It was therefore a joyful surprise to the Board when, at a meeting held in 1861, W. Molson, Esq., announced to his colleagues his intention of building a new wing. The work had scarcely commenced ere he determined to build not only the wing but also the connecting corridors, thus completing the range of buildings according to the original plan, and in the afternoon of the 10th of October, 1862, the "William Molson Hall" was inaugurated in the presence of His Excellency Right Honorable Viscount Monck, Governor General, and a large and brilliant assemblage of officials and citizens.

In the following year (1863) additional advantages were afforded to the students in the organization of a course of Practical Chemistry, under Dr. Sterry Hunt; and by the fall of the same year the Observatory, under Dr. Smallwood, was in full operation. The session which closed in May, 1864, was marked by an event of importance in the history of tbe University, namely, the affiliation of Morrin College, Quebec, which also sent up 11 students, who passed the intermediate examinations. During the same year there was a large increase in the number of medals to be offered to the Graduating Class in Arts. For some years there had been only the medal founded by Mr. Chapman, and subsequently that founded by H. R. H. the Prince of Wales; and the number of rewards being less than that of honor subjects, a certain injustice was done to one or other of these in alternate years. This difficulty was now removed, and in this matter the University was placed on an equality with any other in America. In 1865 the affiliation of the Congregational Theological College of British North America was announced. As the University is constituted it cannot establish a Theological Chair, but Theological Colleges may be affiliated with it, and this was the first step taken towards the full realization of the usefulness of the University as a non-denominational yet Christian institution.

The Congregational College had been engaged under the able management of the Rev. Adam Lillie, D.D., during twenty years, in training a succession of young men for the ministry in the denomination of Christians whose name it bears. Removed to Montreal in 1864, and incorporated by Act of Parliament, it sought and obtained union with the University, in order that its Alumni might have the advantages of the curriculum in the Faculty of Arts, and that it might expend its own strength upon an immediate professional culture. The year 1866 saw the completion of a work which had occupied the attention of the Board of Governors during a period of fifteen years. Their aim had been to render the estate bequeathed by Mr. McGill, productive to the University, and by the skill and care with which they had administered their important trust, a revenue was being derived from the whole of the property, with the exception of the portion necessarily reserved for the College grounds. While this position of comparative financial prosperity was most satisfactory to the friends of the University, still so far as pecuniary means were concerned, the limit of the resources furnished by the McGill endowment had been reached, and the future growth and improvement of the College became dependent on the further benefactions of its friends, and more particularly so from the fact, that there appeared but little hope that the Government of the Province would prove sufficiently just or wise to redeem some of the pledges of public endowment made to the University, and thus remove the reproach of being the only one of the greater colonies of the empire in either the Northern or Southern hemisphere that had made no permanent provision for the support of the higher education. The slow increase of the library was also a cause of solicitude, as it had been from the first the policy of the Governors to endeavour to gather the material of scientific culture and general learning, as well as of the more elementary education of young men. Nothing could, therefore, have proved more acceptable than the gift made by Mr. P. Redpath of a collection of historical works bearing on the history of England, and which was the first donation of a collection of books on any single subject. In 1867 the Museum and Philosophical apparatus received large and valuable additions. The apparatus for experimental physics had for a long time required additions, more especially with reference to the more recent departments of scientific research. To remove this difficulty, seven members of the Board of Governors subscribed the sum of $1,950, and a number of most valuable instruments were procured, thus placing the means of illustration in this department abreast of the requirements of the time.

The museum was also enriched by the liberal donation of the "Carpenter collection" of shells. Dr. Carpenter having brought with him to this country his large and valuable general collection of shells, the result of thirty-three years of labour, and containing materials for the study of recent and fossil Conchology, probably not equalled by any similar collection on this continent, liberally offered to present this collection to the University, on condition that the expense of mounting and arranging the shells, or $2,000, should be defrayed by the University. This offer the Corporation ventured to accept, believing that in doing so it would confer an important benefit on the cause of scientific education and on all students of Zoology and Geology, not only in connection with the University, but throughout the country ; and a subscription was commenced with the view of realizing the sum required, and also a similar sum to provide proper accommodation for the collection in a fire-proof apartment.

During this session the University adopted in the Faculty of Medicine the standard of examinations for matriculation recommended by the Council of Medical Education in Great Britain, thereby raising the standard of the Literary qualifications of candidates for the degree of medicine. In the report of the Board of Governors for the year, reference was made to the fact that no means had been placed at the disposal of the University for affording aids in the way of bursaries and scholarships to deserving students. To those familiar with the importance attached to such stimuli in the mother country and elsewhere, and with the vast sums paid in aids and encouragements to students, it appears surprising that the success achieved by the University had been attained without any of these advantages, and it was evident that could they be provided still greater results might be obtained.

The attention of the public having been directed to this important subject, some were found ready to adopt the suggestion, and Mrs. Redpath, of Terrace Bank, by her liberal gift of $100 annually for an exhibition in the Faculty of Arts, secured the honor of taking the lead in the matter. The example thus set was promptly followed by the members of the Board of Governors who, by a private subscription among themselves, established a scholarship of similar amount. One of the graduates having forwarded a cheque for $100 as an offering of gratitude to his *Alma Mater* from his first professional earning, with the request that it might be employed in the manner most likely to be useful, led to the suggestion that it might be made the nucleus of a Graduate's exhibition. This idea was followed up with success, thus making an era in the history of the University—that in which its own sons return to pour into its own treasury the tribute of their affection and gratitude. While private citizens were thus rendering valuable aid, the Legislature of the Province of Quebec had adopted, with reference to the grants to superior education, a principle which tended to further diminish the slender aids received by the University, under the former Constitution of Canada. A clause of the new Educational Act enacted that all State aids to superior education should be divided into two portions, according to population. Under this arrangement, the English and Protestant minority, who have more important and useful institutions relatively to their numbers, though not relatively to their wealth and intelligence, and to the amount they contribute to the revenue, receive very little assistance from the annual grants, while all the large public endowments, granted by the liberality of past governments, remain in the hands of the majority.

During the many years in which Dr. Dawson has been connected with the University, he has never ceased to urge the importance attached to the establishment of a school of practical science, and many attempts have been made to organize and sustain courses of Engineering and Agriculture, with little success, the limited means of the University not allowing it to sustain the necessary chairs in addition to those of its regular academical course. The liberal benefactions and strenuous efforts in behalf of this object in connection with the Universities of the United States, Great Britain and the Continent of Europe, still more strongly attracted attention to the want of schools of practical science in Canada, and the injury resulting therefrom to the interests of the young men and to the progress of the productive industries of the country.

A committee was accordingly appointed to collect information and to urge upon the Government of the Province of Quebec the importance of extending some assistance at least to Schools of Engineering, Mining, Practical Chemistry and Metallurgy, in connection with the means in aid of such schools already in possession of the University. It was felt by the Corporation that nothing could be more conducive to the material prosperity of the country than the institution of such means of education.

A memorial on this subject was submitted to the Government of Quebec, and Principal Dawson visited some of the most eminent scientific schools in the United States with the view of enabling the Governors to profit by their experience.

On the subject of a school of Mining more especially, the views of the Board were communicated to the Director of the Geological Survey for the information of the Dominion Government ; and the assistance of the University was offered in regard to lectures, class rooms, apparatus, museum, examinations and diplomas, in event of such a school being established in Montreal.

In the meantime the University continued to give, as far as its means permitted, such training in practical geology and allied subjects, as might fit students for entering technical schools of mining.

The Education Bill, passed by the Legislature of Quebec, having apparently terminated all hope of an increased public provision for the higher education in the Province, and the revenues of the University, derived from its private endowments, being barely sufficient for its ordinary expenditure, without permitting any of that growth and extension which are so desirable, it was decided by the Board of Governors again to appeal to the citizens of Montreal, and to endeavour to obtain an additional subscription sufficient to enable the College to retain the remainder of Mr. McGill's estate for College purposes.

This subscription was solicited more especially as an aid to the general funds of the University, or for the endowment of existing chairs, or for scholarships and exhibitions, without excluding any special benefactions for other purposes which might be offered by the friends of education. It was estimated that a capital sum of $150,000 would satisfy all the immediate requirements of the

University and enable it to extend and improve its operations in many very important respects.

Accordingly on the 10th of February, 1870, a meeting of the friends of the University was held, and was attended by a large number of influential citizens. Chancellor Day, in his opening remarks, stated that "an increase of the endowment fund had now become a matter of necessity, and that in the future little was to be expected from the Government. They had done something and might continue to do so for a time, subject, however, to gradual dimunition. There were two means of obtaining an endowment, one of which was the sale of the University Park, which is indispensable to the College, and he believed the citizens would not allow it to be further reduced. The only course to adopt was to apply to the Protestant population, and the meeting had been called to consider how this could be done, and to solicit the aid of those gentlemen present. A few years ago an appeal had been made to the public, and it was followed by such results as showed that they had confidence in the undertaking. He did not think that the people would refuse their aid to an institution which since then had such an honourable career.

The addresses made by others tended to shew that not only were they impressed with the importance of the questions presented, but were determined that strenuous efforts should be at once put forth to relieve the University from its embarrassing position. Resolutions were adopted to the effect—

"That the growth of the country in political importance, and the increase of the Protestant population, has rendered necessary a change and enlargement in the provisions for its advancement in knowledge and mental culture ; and that an increase is required in the means we have hitherto possessed, for giving to our youth a liberal scholastic training."

"That with a view to meet the educational wants above referred to, the present endowment of McGill University ought to be increased so as to place it upon a footing of permanent independence, and enable it to extend its work according to the requirements of the time, and upon an equality with educational institutions abroad."

" That an appeal be made to those interested in the cause of higher education among Protestants, for their aid and contributions toward the important object of increasing the endowment of the McGill College, and that a committee be appointed to take measures for prosecuting such appeal, and for obtaining subscriptions."

The committee appointed in accordance with these resolutions, at once entered upon their duties, and during the year the subscription reached the amount of $57,667, without reckoning sums contributed for scholarships, amounting to $1,900 yearly. Mr. Wm. Molson added to his former gifts a donation of $4,000, to constitute the nucleus of a library fund.

One marked effect of these subscriptions was the stimulus given to students by the scholarships and exhibitions which were instituted. These not only swelled the numbers, but stimulated in a great degree the exertions of students. The prizes also exercise a most healthful effect on the high schools and academies, and enables many young men of ability and industry to secure that higher education which opens up avenues of usefulness and honor for themselves and for their country.

At the meeting held to promote the subscription, a resolution was passed requesting the University to consider the question of the higher education of women. This resolution was not lost sight of, and among those who felt deep interest, none took more active steps than Dr. Dawson toward securing its fulfilment by informing himself of the movements in this direction elsewhere. In the mother country the Universities of Cambridge and Edinburgh had already, through some of their most eminent officers, entered into this work, and classes had also been established successfully in this country, in Toronto, in Kingston and in Quebec.

The McGill University had not received any funds for this purpose, but a subscription was started in 1871 among the lady pupils of the late Miss Lyman to establish a memorial to that eminently useful and gifted lady, in the way she herself would, no doubt, have chosen above all others—a permanent endowment to promote the object for which she labored so long and successfully.

In the meantime an Association was formed for the higher

education of women, on the plan of that in Edinburgh, with the view of providing lectures in the first instance, and eventually of establishing a college for ladies in connection with the University.

In accordance with a decision of the Provisional Committee of this Association, held on the 10th May, 1871, at Belmont Hall, the residence of Mrs. Molson, four courses of lectures were delivered to the members and students of the Association during the session which closed in May, 1872. In addition to the regular instruction, the ladies had the great advantage of two lectures on English history from Professor Goldwin Smith. To these lectures ladies not connected with the Association were admitted by purchased tickets, it being thought right to allow all who desired it the privilege of access. Lectures were also delivered by Prof. P. J. Darey on French Literature, Rev. Prof. Cornish on the English Language, and Dr. T. Sterry Hunt on Chemical and Physical Geology.

The inaugural lecture was delivered by Principal Dawson on the 3rd of October, 1871. The moneys subscribed to the "Hannah Willard Lyman Memorial Fund," is to be annually awarded, as may be recommended by the Governors of the University. For the session of 1872-'73, it is disposed of as follows :—

1. The income to be divided into two equal prizes to be given to the regular students, who having passed creditably in the subjects of examination before Christmas, shall take the highest marks in the first class in the written examinations in one of the subjects at the end of the session.

2. The lecturers to be examiners, and the answers of the successful candidates to be transmitted to the Corporation of the University, with the reports of the examiners.

3. The prizes to be given in books properly inscribed.

The success which attended the first year's working of the Association was very gratifying to those interested, and should the proposed scheme be carried out for the erection in the course of a few years of a college for ladies, where an academical course can be pursued suitable to themselves and different in some respects from that taken by ordinary college students, there can be no doubt that the advantages afforded to ladies anxious to follow the higher branches of study will be very great.

In 1871, the High School was transferred by the Governors of the University to the Protestant Board of School Commissioners for the city of Montreal. For 18 years this school had been efficiently carried on under the direction of the University, and many of the pupils had passed therefrom to the College and had graduated with the highest honors. Since assuming charge of the school, the Commissioners have sustained its reputation.

During this year a plan for the establishing of a department of Practical Science was laid before the public, and an impetus was given to the same by a liberal donation of $5,000 from Daniel Torrance, Esq., of New York.

The courses of study in this Department are designed to afford a complete preliminary training of a Technical as well as a Theoretical nature, for such students as are preparing to enter any of the various branches of the professions of Engineering and Surveying, or are destined to be engaged in Assaying, Practical Chemistry and the higher forms of Manufacturing Art.

Three distinct courses of study are provided, each of which extends over three, or under certain conditions two years, and specially adapted to the prospective pursuits of the student.

(1) Civil and Mechanical Engineering.
(2) Assaying and Mining.
(3) Practical Chemistry.

The Degrees conferred by the University upon such Undergraduates of this Department as shall fulfil the conditions and pass the examinations are in the first instance " Bachelor of Applied Science," mention being made in the Diplomas of the particular course of study pursued; and subsequently the degrees of " Master of Engineering " on those who have pursued Course 1st, and of " Master of Applied Science " on those who have pursued either of the remaining courses.

In 1872, the Caledonian Society inaugurated a movement towards founding a " Scott Bursary Fund," to substantially commemorate the Scott centenary. The sum of $1,100 was subscribed and handed over to the College, to be invested as a fund for the establishment of an exhibition of English Literature, and is now open to students in the Department of Science who have passed the examinations of the middle year. Sir Wm. Logan, also, by a

MOLSON.

gift of $20,000, endowed a chair of Geology, to be known as the Logan Chair, and at the same time named Principal Dawson as the first Logan Professor. This munificent act was the closing event of importance in the history of the University.

Mr. McGill's bequest has been the foundation upon which, in various ways, has been built up an Institution second to none in the Province for the numbers it educates and the aid it affords to the growing intelligence of a large portion of the population. Alone, that bequest, munificent as it was, was inadequate to such a result. But it has awakened the zeal and stimulated the efforts of others, and produced a kindred generosity which has shown itself in the unstinted contributions already noticed.

The support which the University has received from the citizens of Montreal is not without significance and high promise. It shows them to be men not penurious and locally selfish, but nobly generous in their views; and the fact that so many hundreds of young men from all parts of Canada have enjoyed, and are enjoying, the benefits of their liberality, has in it a double promise of more liberal and united public sentiment in Canada for the time to come. Further, the interest which the business men of this commercial metropolis take in the work is an evidence of its practical value, and a pledge that in this country the higher learning will not be dissociated from the active pursuits of life. Still further, it marks the McGill University as a spontaneous growth of the British Canadian mind, — something which has originated here, and been nurtured and matured here, and not a thing of extraneous origin.

In its religious aspect the University is not denominational. It does not profess to work for one body of Christians more than for another. But it is Christian and Protestant. The Anglican, the Catholic, the Protestant dissenter of whatever name, and the Israelite, here meet on a footing of the most perfect equality. It is neither a proselytizing institution on the one hand, nor an irreligious one on the other. It endeavours to secure the services of men of high religious and moral character, and to exercise through them the best influence on its students. It daily invites its students to supplicate the Divine blessing on their work, and it requires them to avail themselves of the means of spiritual advantage to be found in their several communions. Its influence is thus positively religious, and is exercised in such a way as to unite the members of different denominations in love and harmony.

A measure of the success attending the College is due to the assiduous devotion and good judgment of the gentleman who fills the position of Principal and Vice-Chancellor, on whom the immediate educational management devolves. While his administration of the affairs of the College has demanded the greater portion of his time, Dr. Dawson has, nevertheless, won for himself a widespread fame as an author of several scientific works of great value, beside a number of essays published in the transactions of scientific bodies, or in pamphlet form.

Faculty of Medicine.

About the year 1823, conscious of the want, experienced in this Province by Medical Students, of lectures on the different branches of Medical study, Dr. A. F. Holmes, together with Drs. Robertson, Stephenson, and Caldwell, organized themselves into a body, and, under the name of the Medical Institution of Montreal, they delivered, for the first time in 1824, forming the session of 1824-'25, a course of lectures, which were recognized by the University of Edinburgh afterwards, on the principle of two courses for one of that University. In 1828 this Institution became merged into the University of McGill College. The first lectures were delivered as follows :—Dr. Holmes, on Chemistry and Materia Medica ; Dr. Stephenson, on Anatomy, Physiology, and Surgery ; Dr. Robertson, on Midwifery and the diseases of women and children ; and Dr. Caldwell, on the Principles and Practice of Medicine. The death of Dr. Caldwell in 1832, necessitated a change and Dr. Robertson was appointed Professor of Medicine, while Dr. Racey was annexed as Professor of Surgery and Midwifery, Dr. Stephenson still continuing to discharge the duties of the Chair of Anatomy and Physiology. On the retirement of Dr. Racey from Montreal to Quebec in 1835, Drs. Geo. W. Campbell and Hall were associated, the former lecturing independently on Surgery and Midwifery, and the latter sharing Dr. Holmes' duties and delivering under him the course of Materia Medica, after which session that course was delivered over exclusively to the latter.

During this period of time the annual attendance of students was gradually augmenting, and the fact, together with the further division of the branches of Medical study in Great Britain, determined at the decease of Dr. Robertson in 1844, a further augmentation of lectures correspondent with an increased number of Chairs. We accordingly find at this juncture, Dr. Holmes called to the Chair of the Principles and Practice of Medicine; Dr. Chas. Sewell, appointed to the Chair of Materia Medica ; Dr. Bruneau, to the Chair of Anatomy ; Dr. Hall, to the Chair of Chemistry ; Dr. Crawford, to that of Clinical Medicine and

Surgery ; Dr. McCulloch, to that of Midwifery ; and Dr. Fraser, to that of Institutes of Medicine, while Dr. Campbell still retained his Chair of Surgery. Since that period several changes and additions have been made, as appears in the staff of Professors at present. At the new organization of the University, Dr. Holmes was appointed Dean of the Faculty, and he continued to discharge, until the day of his death, (October 9, 1860,) the various duties which devolved upon him with a rare fidelity. Dr. G. W. Campbell became his successor and still continues to fill the position for which he is eminently qualified and which is unquestionably his due from his long and faithful services to the Faculty.

McGill University having been included among the Universities recognized by the Medical Council of Great Britain and Ireland, its degree has accordingly been registered by that Council, thereby conferring upon graduates of the University the same privileges as Physicians or Surgeons of Great Britain.

The class tickets for the various courses are accepted as qualifying candidates for examination before the Universities and Colleges of Great Britain and Ireland, and also before the Medical Boards of the Army and Navy.

To meet the circumstances of General Practitioners in British North America, where there is no division of the profession into Physicians and Surgeons exclusively, the degree awarded upon graduation is that of "Doctor of Medicine and Master in Surgery." This designation is also appropriate, from agreeing with the general nature and equable character of the previous curriculum demanded of the candidates for this double rank. The degree is received by the College of Physicians and Surgeons of Lower Canada, and by the Council of Medical Education and Registration of Upper Canada.

The ample and varied means which are placed at the disposal of the student by this school, together with the large hospitals in connection with it, render it second to no Medical School in America.

The Library contains upwards of 4,000 volumes, including the most useful books for reference, as well as the most elementary ones ; the works of the older authors as well as the most recent.

It is open to the Students without charge, under necessary regulations for the care of books. The Museum contains a large number of preparations, chiefly Pathological ; also, wax and papier maché models.

The Montreal General Hospital is visited every day by the Medical Officers in attendance. After the visit a large number of out-door patients are examined and prescribed for.

The Operating Room (used also for a lecture room) is so constructed as to suit the convenience of the students in obtaining a good view of the operations going on.

The University Lying-in-Hospital is under the direction of the Professor of Midwifery. Students who have already attended one course of his lectures are furnished with cases in rotation.

The Medical Faculty Prizes consist, first of the Holmes Gold Medal, founded by the Faculty in honor of their late Dean, and two prizes in Books for the best Primary and best Final Graduation Examination.

The building, at present occupied, has been for many years too limited, and there is now in course of erection on the College grounds a building suited in every particular and specially designed to furnish ample accommodation for the rapidly increasing number of students who flock to this popular School of Medicine.

Medals.

Gold medals are but the gilding on the surface of a college education, but they stimulate to a healthy emulation, and give to deserving young men a memorial of early triumphs and an earnest of success in life.

For many years McGill College had no such distinctions to offer; but this difficulty has been removed, and it can now take its place on an equality with any American University.

First in order of time, a merchant of Montreal, Henry Chapman, Esq., founded (1857) a Gold Medal for an honor course in Classical Literature and Languages. This medal has on its obverse the God of Labor, with the motto: " *Vere novo terra colenda est,*" and in exergue " *Grandescunt aucta labore.*" Reverse : A wreath of laurel with College arms at the top. Inside of wreath, " *Henricus Chapman, donavit.*" Outside : " *Universitas Collegii McGill Monte Regio.*"

In 1860, His Royal Highness the Prince of Wales, among other donations, handed over to the College authorities the sum of £200, which was applied to the foundation of a Gold Medal, to be called the " Prince of Wales Gold Medal." This medal is for an honor course in Logic and Mental and Moral Philosophy. Obverse : Head to right — " *Albertus Edvardus artium liberalium fautor canada visa D.* 1860." Reverse : Arms of College with maple and oak wreath—" *Universitas McGill Monte Regio.*"

In 1864, Mrs. Molson offered to the University a Gold Medal for Mathematics and Physical Sciences, and the " Anne Molson Medal " forms a graceful link of connection with the College to a name already noted for liberality. More than this, as coming from a lady's hand, it is a mark of the interest which an educated and thoughtful woman takes in the higher education, and of the sympathy which a mother feels with the struggles of the sons of other Canadian mothers to earn honourable distinction. This medal is of the following design : Obverse—Head of Newton to the left—" *Scientiis Mathematicis et Physicis Feliciter excultis.*" Reverse : A laurel wreath, between the top leaves of which are the Molson arms (a shield bearing

LOGAN.

TORRANCE.

six crescents). In centre of wreath — "*Anna Molson donavit.*" Outside of wreath — "*Universitas McGill Monte Regio.*" "*In domino confido.*"

It has often been said, though little followed in practice, that when we are called on to celebrate the memory of the mighty dead, we do this in the most rational and most fitting way by helping and succouring their living representatives and successors, by promoting the ends to which they devoted their lives, and by striving ourselves and stimulating others to imitate whatever was good or great in their examples. These were evidently the views of those citizens of Montreal who founded the " THE SHAKSPERE MEDAL." Whether regarded as an evidence of affection for the University, as an inducement to the culture of our noble English tongue, or as a means of honouring the memory of the great dramatist, or as uniting all these motives and objects, it was most honourable to them, and deserves to be widely known as one of the happiest thoughts that occurred to any community in connection with the Shakspere ter-centenary celebration. The design chosen for this medal presents on the obverse a fine portrait of Shakspere, with the simple inscription " *Shakspere*, 1564—1616." The reverse bears a richly ornamented shield, with the College arms above, and in the centre, " *Shakspere ter centenary* 1864." A ribbon which extends across the lower part of the shield is inscribed " *For English Literature.*" On the outer circle surrounding the shield appears the title—" *McGill College, Montreal.*"

Not less appropriate was the foundation of " THE LOGAN MEDAL " for Geology and Natural Science, which will forever connect the name of the great Canadian geologist, a name itself imperishable, with the successive aspirants to distinction in the same honourable path who go forth from the University, and who may uphold the reputation of this country in a subject in itself second to no department of scientific study, and which is one of the most important to the educated Canadian, and offers, more than any other, avenues to scientific distinction and eminence. The obverse bears a portrait of the donor, and the inscription— " *Gulielmus E. Logan Eques.* The reverse displays the College arms between the top leaves of a maple wreath, within which is inscribed—" *Universitas McGill Monte Regio,*" while on the outer edge of the medal is placed the following—"*Ad Geologiam et Scientias Naturales excolendas Gul E. Logan eq. D.* 1864."

In the following year (1865), the late John Torrance, Esq., of St. Antoine Hall, Montreal, founded, in memory of his wife, a medal to be known as the "ELIZABETH TORRANCE GOLD MEDAL," for the best student of the graduating class in law, and more especially for the highest proficiency in Roman law. It was but natural that this medal should be given to the department of law as a member of the family, Judge F. W. Torrance held for many years the professorship of Roman law in connection with the College. The design chosen for this medal is exceedingly appropriate. A full face bust of Justinian with an ancient Roll appears on the obverse, and above the bust is the name "*Justinianus,*" while on the reverse are two palm branches encircling the words "*Universitas McGill, Præmium in facultate juris.*" On a ribbon which almost surrounds the medal is the inscription— "*Ad nom Elizabeth Torrance perpetuand marit Joannes Torrance Inst.* 1864."

During the same year the Faculty of Medicine founded a medal in honor of the late Dean, Professor Holmes, of whom it may be said that no man lived more conscientiously, and few have died more beloved. This medal is a most deserving and grateful tribute to the memory of departed worth, associated as it is with the name of one who was the founder of the first medical school in Canada, and who, for nearly forty years, remained in connection therewith. The medal is given, annually, to the best student in the graduating class in Medicine who shall undergo a special examination in all the branches, whether primary or final. On the obverse of the medal is the head of Hippocrates with the named ΙΠΠΟΚΡΑΤΣ to the left. Reverse : The arms of the College, and a wreath of laurel enclosing the words "*Facultas medicinæ donavit,*" and encircling the whole is the inscription "*In memoriam Andreæ F. Holmes, M.D., LL.D.*"

In addition to these there are also two medals awarded to students in the High School and the Normal Schools. The former is an annual gift from D. Davidson, Esq., of Edinburgh, (formerly of Montreal). Owing to the altered circumstances of the school, it is doubtful whether Mr. Davidson will continue the gift. It is, however, to be hoped that he may yet decide to offer the same as an incentive to those who may enter upon the course of study prescribed by this school. The medal bears on the obverse—Minerva's head, and the motto : " *Nil sine magno labore.*" Reverse : A wreath of laurel encircling the inscription " *Hoc præmium ingenii bene culti Regiæ scholæ montis regalis donavit D. Davidson tulit.*"

A medal known as " THE PRINCE OF WALES BRONZE MEDAL " is provided for by a gift of His Royal Highness the Prince of Wales, and is awarded to students in the Normal Schools of Lower Canada. It bears on the obverse a bust of the Prince, and on the reverse—" *Edvardus Albertus princeps cambriæ provinciam Canadensam fausta præsentia honoratam perlustrans in unaquaque normali schola præmium in singolos annos munifice in stituit A.D. MDCCCLX in* . . . . *schola* . . . . *mer et cons A.D.* 18 ."

BENEFACTORS OF THE UNIVERSITY.

Original Endowment by last will and testament of Hon. Jas. McGill under date 8th January, 1811. The value of property thus bequeathed being estimated at the date of the bequest at £30,000.

SUBSCRIPTIONS TO ENDOWMENT FUND, 1856.

The Hon. John Molson, }	John James Day, Esq. - - 150
Thomas Molson, Esq., } £25,000	Thos. Brown Anderson, Esq. 150
William Molson, Esq., }	Peter Redpath, Esq. - - 150
for the formation and	Thomas M. Taylor, Esq. - 150
maintenance of the chair	Joseph McKay, Esq. - - 150
of English Language and	Donald Lorn McDougall, Esq. 150
Literature.	Honorable John Rose, - 150
John Gordon McKenzie, Esq. 500	Charles Alexander, Esq. - 150
Ira Gould, Esq. - 500	Moses E. David, Esq. - - 150
John Frothingham, Esq. - 500	Wm. Carter, Esq. - - 150
John Torrance, Esq. - - 500	Thomas Patton, Esq. - 150
James B. Greenshields, Esq. 300	Wm. Workman, Esq. - - 150
William Busby Lambe. Esq. - 300	Honorable A. T. Galt, - - 150
Sir George Simpson, Knight, 250	Honorable Luther H. Holton, 150
Henry Thomas, Esq. - 250	Henry Lyman, Esq. - - 150
John Redpath, Esq. - - 250	David Torrance, Esq. - 150
James McDougall, Esq. - 250	Edwin Atwater, Esq. - - 150
James Torrance, Esq. - 250	Theodore Hart, Esq. - - 150
Honorable James Ferrier, - 250	William Forsyth Grant, Esq. - 150
John Smith, Esq. - - 250	Robert Campbell, Esq. - 150
Harrison Stephens, Esq. - 250	Alfred Savage, Esq. - - 150
James Mitchell, Esq. - 250	James Ferrier, jr., Esq. - 150
Henry Chapman, Esq. - - 150	William Stephens, Esq. - - 150
	N. S. Whitney, Esq, 150
Mr. Chapman also founded a	William Dow, Esq. - 150
Gold Medal to be given an-	William Watson, Esq. 150
nually in the graduating	Edward Major, Esq. - - 150
class in Arts.	Hon. Charles Dewey Day, 50
Honorable Peter McGill, - 150	John R. Esdaile, Esq. - 50

WILLIAM MOLSON HALL.

Being the West wing of the College Buildings, with the Museum Rooms, and the Chemical Laboratory and Class Rooms, was erected in 1861 through the munificent donation of the founder whose name it bears.

EXHIBITIONS AND SCHOLARSHIPS IN ARTS.

The "Jane Redpath Exhibition," $100 annually, was founded in 1868 by Mrs. Redpath, of Terrace Bank, Montreal, and endowed with the sum of $1,667.

The Governors' Scholarship of $100 to $120 annually, was founded by subscription of members of the Board of Governors in 1869.

The Scott Exhibition founded by the Caledonian Society of Montreal, in commemoration of the Centenary of Sir Walter Scott, and endowed in 1872 with the sum of $1,100 subscribed by members of the Society, and other citizens of Montreal. The Exhibition is given annually in the Department of practical and applied Science.

There are eleven other Scholarships and Exhibitions, for which see "Subscription in Progress."

MISCELLANEOUS SUBSCRIPTIONS.

Mrs. G. Frothingham, for the arrangement of Dr. Carpenter's Collection of Mazatlan Shells, - - - - $233

Hon. C. Dunkin, M.P., in aid of the chair of Practical Chemistry, - - - 1,200

Principal Dawson in aid of the same, - - - 1,200

P. Redpath, Esq., do. do. 266

Subscriptions for the purchase of Philosophical Apparatus, 1867 :

William Molson, Esq.	$500	
J. H. R. Molson, Esq.	500	
Peter Redpath, Esq.	500	
George Moffat, Esq.	250	2,050
Andrew Robertson, Esq.	100	
John Frothingham, Esq.	100	
David Torrance, Esq.	100	

Subscriptions for the erection of a Fire-proof Building for the Carpenter Collection of shells, 1868.

Peter Redpath, Esq. - -	$500
William Molson, Esq. -	500
H. Stephens, Esq. - -	100
R. J. Reekie, Esq. - -	100
J. H. R. Molson, Esq. - -	100
Sir W. E. Logan, F.R.S. -	100
J. Molson, Esq. - -	100
Thomas Workman, Esq., M.P.	100
G. Frothingham, Esq. - -	100
Wm. Dow, Esq. - -	$100
Thomas Rimmer, Esq. - -	100

Andrew Robertson, Esq. -	100
Mrs. Redpath, - -	100
Benaiah Gibb, Esq. -	50
Honorable John Rose, -	30
	$2,180

Subscriptions for the erection of the Lodge and gates.

William Molson, Esq. - -	100
John H. R. Molson, Esq.	100
William Workman, Esq. -	100
Joseph Tiffin, jr., Esq. -	100
T. James Claxton, Esq. -	100
James Linton, Esq. - -	100
William MacDougall, Esq. -	100
Charles J. Brydges, Esq. -	100
George Drummond, Esq. -	100
Thomas Rimmer, Esq. -	100
William Dow, Esq. - -	100
John Frothingham, Esq. -	100
James A. Mathewson, Esq. -	100
Peter Redpath, Esq. - -	$100
G. H. Frothingham, Esq.	100
G. D. Ferrier, Esq. - -	100
Geo. W. Warner, Esq. -	100
John Smith, Esq. - -	100
Charles Alexander, Esq. -	100
J. E. Evans, Esq. - -	100
Henry Lyman, Esq. -	50
	$2050.00

T. M. Thomson, Esq., for five prizes in the Faculty of Arts in the Session 1869-'70, - - - $250

Subscription in Progress.

Peter Redpath, Esq., for the Endowment of the Chair of Natural Philosophy, **$20,000**

Sir W. E. Logan, LL.D., F.R.S. the sum of $19,000, and Hart Logan, Esq., the sum of $1000, for the Endowment of the "Logan chair of Geology." - - - - **20,000**

William Molson, Esq. - - **5,000**

W. C. McDonald, Esq. - **5,000**

Mr. McDonald gives also $1,250 yearly for the maintenance of ten Scholarships and Exhibitions of the annual value of $125 each.

Thomas Workman, Esq. - **5,000**

John Frothingham, Esq. **5,000**

J. H. R. Molson, Esq. - - **2,000**

Charles Alexander, Esq., for the endowment of a Scholarship of the annual value of $120, - - - **2,000**

Honorable F. W. Torrance, **1,000**

G. W. Campbell, Esq., M.D. **$1,000**

B. Gibb, Esq. - - **600**

W. Notman, Esq. - - **600**

T. W. Ritchie, Esq. - **600**

A. & W. Robertson, Esqrs. **600**

T. M. Taylor, Esq., $100 per annum for a Scholarship.

T. M. Thomsom, Esq., $200 for two Exhibitions in September, 1871, **200**

T. J. Claxton, Esq., £50 sterling for additions to the Museum, - - **250**

John Reddy, Esq., M.D. **100**

Messrs. Sinclair, Jack & Co. **250**

Wm. Lunn, Esq. - - **100**

Kenneth Campbell, Esq. **100**

William Rae, Esq. - - **50**

John McLennan, Esq. - **1,000**

R. A. Ramsay, Esq. - **100**

Wm. Molson, Esq., for Library Fund, - - **4,000**

Endowment for Special Objects, held in trust by the Board of the Royal Institution.

The "Hannah Willard Lyman Memorial Fund" contributed by subscription of former pupils of Miss Lyman, and invested as a permanent Endowment, to furnish annually a Scholarship or Prize in a College for Women affiliated to the University, or in Classes for the Higher Education of Women approved by the University. The amount of the fund is at present $940.

Special Endowment for Department of Practical Science.

David Torrance, Esq. - - - - - - - **$5,000**

George Moffatt, Esq. - - - - - - **1,000**

C. J. Brydges, Esq. - - - - - - **1,000**

R. J. Reekie, Esq. - - - - - - **1,000**

Hon. James Ferrier, (per annum for seven years) - - - **100**

Donald Ross, Esq. do. do. - - - **50**

P. Redpath, Esq., (per annum for five years) - - - **400**

J. H. R. Molson, Esq., do. - - - **400**

G. H. Frothingham, Esq., do. - - - **400**

T. James Claxton, Esq., (per annum) - - - - - **100**

Charles Gibb, B.A., donation for apparatus- - **50**

HOLMES.

NIL SINE MAGNO LABORE

DAVIDSON.
HIGH SCHOOL

Officers of Instruction.

John William Dawson, LL.D., F.R.S., F.G.S.—Principal, Logan Professor of Geology, and Professor of Natural History.

Ven. Archdeacon Leach, D.C.L., LL.D.—Vice-Principal, Dean of the Faculty of Arts, and Molson Professor of English Literature.

Henry Aspinwall Howe, LL.D.—Emeritus Professor of Mathematics and Natural Philosophy.

Hon. J. J. C. Abbott, D.C.L.—Dean of the Faculty of Law, and Professor of Commercial Law.

George W. Campbell, M.A., M.D.—Dean of the Faculty of Medicine and Professor of Surgery.

William Fraser, M.D.—Professor of the Institutes of Medicine.

William Sutherland, M.D.—Emeritus Professor in the Faculty of Medicine.

William E. Scott, M.D.—Professor of Anatomy.

William Wright, M.D.—Professor of Materia Medica and Pharmacy.

Robert P. Howard, M.D.—Professor of the Theory and Practice of Medicine.

Rev. A. DeSola, LL.D.—Professor of Hebrew and Oriental Literature.

Hon. William Badgeley, D.C.L.—Professor of Public and Criminal Law.

P. R. Lafrenaye, B.C.L.—Professor of Legal History.

R. G. Laflamme, B.C.L.—Professor of the Law of Real Estate.

Charles Smallwood, M.D., LL.D., D.C.L.—Professor of Meteorology.

Charles F. A. Markgraf, M.A.—Prof. of German Language and Literature.

D. C. McCallum, M.D.—Professor of Midwifery and Diseases of Women and Children.

Alexander Johnson, LL.D.—Professor of Mathematics, and Redpath Professor of Natural Philosophy.

Rev. George Cornish, LL.D.—Professor of Classical Literature.

Pierre J. Darey, M.A.,B.C.L.—Professor of French Language and Literature.

Robert Craik, M.D.—Professor of Chemistry.

Edward Carter, Q.C., B.C.L.—Associate Professor of Criminal Law.

G. E. Fenwick, M.D.—Professor of Clinical Surgery and Medical Jurisprudence.

Joseph M. Drake, M.D.—Professor of Clinical Medicine.

N. W. Trenholme, M.A., B.C.L.—Professor of Roman Law.

J. S. C. Wurtele, B.C.L.—Associate Professor of Commercial Law.

William H. Kerr, Esq.—Professor of International Law.

Gonzalve Doutre, B.C.L.—Professor of Civil Procedure.

George F. Armstrong, M.A., C.E., F.G.S.—Professor of Civil Engineering and Applied Mechanics.

Gilbert P. Girdwood, M.D.—Professor of Practical Chemistry.

Rev. J. Clarke Murray.—Professor of Logic, Mental and Moral Philosophy.

Lecturers.

John S. Archibald, B.A., B.C.L.—Lecturer in Criminal Law.

Bernard L. Harrington, B.A., Ph.D.—Lecturer in Assaying, Mining and Chemistry.

William Fuller, M.D.—Demonstrator of Anatomy.

———

John Andrew—Instructor in Elocution.

Frederick S. Barnjum—Instructor in Gymnastics.

Affiliated Colleges & Schools.

Students are matriculated in the University, and may pursue their course of study, wholly in the affiliated College, or in part therein, and in part in McGill College, and may come up to the University Examinations on the same terms with the students of McGill College. Affiliated Theological Colleges have the right of obtaining for their students the advantage, in whole or in part, of the course of study in arts, with such facilities in regard to exemptions as may be agreed on.

Morrin College.

So called in honor of its Founder, is situated at Quebec, and is affiliated in so far as regards degrees in arts and laws.

St. Francis College.

Is affiliated in so far as regards degrees in art. The College is situated in Richmond, Township of Cleveland, Quebec.

The object of the Institution is to furnish facilities for lads and young men to procure a thorough education. It comprises a Collegiate and a Preparatory Department. The College Course requires 4 years time, and embraces all the branches usually pursued in other Colleges.

There is also a scientific course of 3 years, including all the studies of the former, except the classics.

In the Preparatory Department are included those branches usually required to fit young men for college, for teaching elementary schools, or for business.

The entire Institution is under the immediate management of the Faculty, subject to the approval of a Board of Trustees.

CONGREGATIONAL COLLEGE OF BRITISH NORTH AMERICA.

This institution was formally opened at Toronto on the 1st September, 1840. The original name borne by it was "The Congregational Academy," and it was under the joint management of the Colonial Missionary Society and the Congregational Union of Canada West. In 1842, the Union of Canada East resolved to establish a "Congregational Institute of Eastern Canada," at Montreal, embracing the two objects of a superior education on Christian principles, and of training suitable young men for the ministry. Committees of management were appointed, and Revs. Drs. Carruthers (subsequently of Portland, Maine), and Wilkes, were chosen Professors. In 1845, negotiations were opened with the sub-committee for the Academy of the Union of Canada West, for a junction of the two institutions. The latter body acceded to the proposal, and in 1846 a Constitution prepared by the Committee in Toronto was accepted by the two Unions, and the name was changed to "The Canadian Congregational Theological Institute." In 1860 another change was made. The Union of Nova Scotia and New Brunswick having begun to look to Canada for a supply of ministers, and "Gorham College" at Liverpool, N.S., having been closed, the name was changed to that by which it is now known, and other alterations made, pertaining chiefly to the course of study. In 1865 the College removed to Montreal, and affiliated with McGill College. Rev. Dr. Lillie, who, throughout a period of nearly 30 years, had been at the head of the professional staff, died at Montreal in 1869, and was succeeded by Dr. Wilkes as Professor of Theology, Homiletics and Church History, Rev. Dr. Cornish being Professor of Greek, &c. The devotion of Dr. Cornish to the interests of the College is shewn by the fact that his services are rendered gratuitously.

At present the sessions of the College are held in the class rooms added for that purpose to Zion Church.

THE PRESBYTERIAN COLLEGE OF MONTREAL,

In connection with the Canada Presbyterian Church,

was established in 1868, and thus far the hopes entertained by its founders have been fully realized; the work of the church in the Province having been greatly strengthened and extended. The attendance of students has been satisfactory, and during the College sessions they render most valuable services in the city and vicinity.

Hitherto the work of the College has been carried on in rooms in Erskine Church, the use of which has been kindly granted by its managers. In view of the steady growth of the institution, and the urgent necessity of providing proper facilities for its work, its friends and supporters recently resolved to do two things: First — To provide for the support of an additional Chair in Theology; Second—To erect College buildings.

A liberal amount has already been secured towards the salary of an additional professor. A most eligible site on McTavish street, adjoining McGill College, has been purchased, and plans procured, by which it appears that the cost of grounds and building will not be less than thirty thousand dollars, of which a large proportion has already been subscribed. The building is now in course of erection. It is a stone edifice, elegant, and in all respects commodious and most pleasantly situated, and commanding a view of the city, the scenery of the St. Lawrence, and the country to the south of it. It contains Lecture Rooms, Library, Examination Hall, Reading Room, Studies and Dormitories for students, together with Bath Rooms, and all other modern conveniences. The rooms will be furnished and given to students free of expense, thus reducing the cost of living to the minimum. During the last session 18 scholarships were competed for, 14 of which were offered by residents of Montreal, and the students have, at their own expense, founded a Gold Medal to be offered for competition annually to the members of the graduating class, the nature of the examination to be determined by the Senate, and to embrace a wide range of theological and kindred subjects.

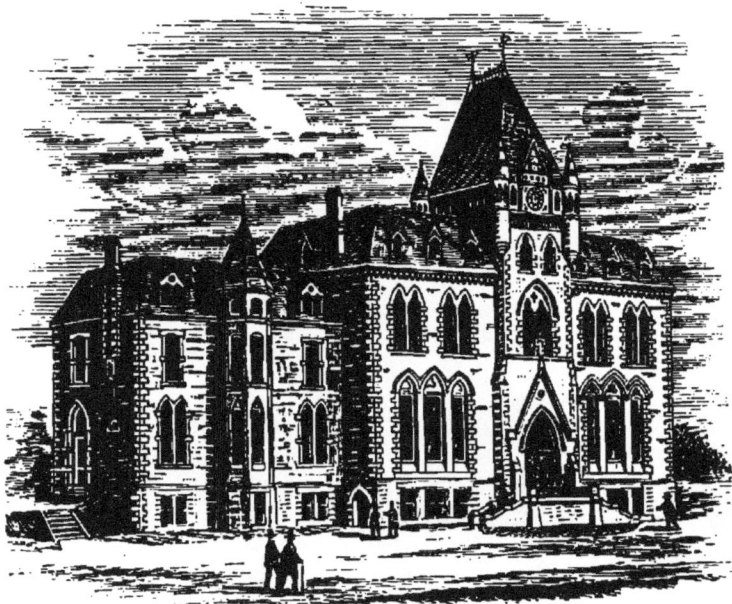

PRESBYTERIAN COLLEGE.

The medal will not be awarded unless a high standard of excellence is attained.

The design for this medal has not yet been decided upon. It is certain, however, that it will compare favorably with the beautiful medals awarded by McGill College.

The officers of instruction are Rev. D. H. MacVicar, LL.D., Professor of Systematic Theology and Apologetics.

Rev. D. Coussirat, B.D., Professor of Dogmatics, Philosophy, &c. (Lectures in French.)

Rev. J. M. Gibson, M.A., Lecturer in Exegetics.

G. Gibson, M.A., Classical and Mathematical Tutor.

Hebrew is taught by Rev. Prof. A. DeSola, LL.D., of McGill College, who also gives instruction in Chaldee, Syriac and Arabic, if required.

Other subjects of the curriculum have been hitherto provided for by special arrangements, but the staff of instructors is to be increased before next session.

McGill Normal School.

Established—1856.

Under the Regulations for the establishment of Normal Schools in the Province of Quebec, the Minister of Public Instruction is empowered to associate with himself for the Direction of one of these Schools the Corporation of McGill University, Montreal. In accordance with this arrangement the Provincial Protestant Normal School is affiliated with the McGill University.

This institution is intended to give a thorough training to teachers, especially for the Protestant population of Lower Canada. This end is attained by instruction and training in the Normal School itself, and by practice in the Model Schools; and the arrangements are of such a character as to afford the greatest possible facilities to students from all parts of the Province.

The complete course of study extends over three years, and the students are graded as follows :—

1. *Elementary School Class.*— Studying for the Elementary School Diploma.

2. *Model School Class.*—Studying for the Model School Diploma.

3. *Academy Class.*—Studying for the Academy Diploma.

Each student must produce a certificate of good moral character from the clergyman or minister of religion under whose charge he has last been, and also testimony that he has attained the age of sixteen years. He is also required to sign a pledge that he purposes to teach for three years in some public school in Lower Canada.

At the close of the first year of study, students may apply for examination for diplomas giving the right to teach in Elementary Schools ; and after two years' study, or if found qualified at the close of the first year, they are, on examination, entitled to diplomas as teachers of Model Schools.

Students having passed the examination in the Model School Class, or having advanced to the requisite knowledge, may go on to the Academy Class, and, on examination, may obtain the Academy Diploma.

MODEL SCHOOL OF MCGILL NORMAL SCHOOL.

These Schools can accommodate about 300 pupils, and are supplied with the best furniture and apparatus, and conducted on the most modern methods of teaching. They receive pupils from the age of six and upwards, and give a thorough English education.

Graduates of the University.

Doctors of Divinity.

Bethune, Rev. John, (ad eundem). 1843 | *Falloon, Rev. Daniel, [Hon.]...... 1844

Doctors of Laws and of Civil Laws.

Abbott, Christopher, B.C.L. [D.C.L. in course]................. 1862
Abbott, Hon. J. J. C., B.C.L. [D.C.L. in course]................ 1867
Adamson, Rev. Wm. A. [D.C.L. hon] 1850
Badgley, Hon. Wm. [D.C.L. hon.]... 1843
Bancroft, Rev. C., D.D. [LL.D. hon] 1870
Bond, Rev. Wm., M.A., [LL.D. hon] 1870
Browne, Dunbar. M. A., B. C. L., [D.C.L. in course]............. 1871
Chamberlin, B., M.A.,B.C.L.[D.C.L. in course].................. 1867
Chauveau, Hon. Pierre J. O. [LL.D. hon.]....................... 1857
Cordner, Rev. John. LL.D. hon.].. 1870
Cornish, Rev. George, M.A., [LL.D. in course]................. 1872
Davies, Rev.Benjamin, Ph.D.[LL.D. hon.]........................ 1856
Dawson, John William, M.A.[LL.D. hon.]........................ 1857
DeSola. Rev. A., [LL.D. hon.]...... 1858
Douglas, Rev. Geo.. [LL.D. hon.].. 1870
*Falloon. Rev. D., D.D.. [LL.D. hon] 1862
*Head. Right Hon. Sir Edmund W., Baronet, M.A.. [LL.D. hon.].... 1863
Hemming. Edward J., B.C.L.[D.C.L. in course.].................. 1871

*Holmes, Andrew F., M.D., [LL.D. hon.]......................... 1858
Howe, Henry A., M.A., [LL.D. hon.] 1870
Hunt, Sterry T.. M.A. [LL.D. hon.] 1865
Lawson, G., Ph.D. [LL.D. hon.].... 1862
Leach. Rev. Wm. T., M.A., [D.C.L. hon.]........................ 1849
[LL.D.hon].................... 1857
Logan. Sir Wm. E. Kt., [LL.D. hon.] 1856
*Lundy, Rev. Francis, [D.C.L, hon.] 1843
Lyall, Rev. W., [LL.D. hon.]....... 1864
McVicar, Rev. D. H., [LL.D. hon.].. 1870
Meredith, Edmund A., B.C.L., [LL.D. hon]..................... 1857
Miles. Hy. H.. M.A., [LL.D. hon.].. 1866
Morris, Alexander, M.A., B.C.L. [D.C.L. in course]............ 1862
Rollitt. Albert. K., LL.D., London Univ. [LL.D. ad eun.]......... 1871
Smallwood, Charles. M.D. [LL.D. hon.]......................... 1856
*Smith. William, [LL.D. hon.]..... 1858
*Valieres de St. Real, Hon. J. R., [D.C.L. hon.].............. 1844
Wickes, Rev. W. D.. [LL.D. hon.].. 1868
Wilkes. Rev. Henry, D.D., M.A., [LL.D. hon.]................... 1870

Doctors of Medicine.

Adsetts, John...................... 1866
Alexander Robt. A................. 1871
Allen. Hamilton................... 1872
Alloway, Thomas Johnson........... 1869
Anderson, Alexander............... 1866
Anderson, John C.................. 1865
Archer, Thomas.................... 1869
Ardagh, Johnson................... 1869
*Arnoldi, Daniel, [Hon.].......... 1847
Atkinson, Robt.................... 1862
Ault, Alexander................... 1860
Ault, Charles..................... 1855
Ault. James F..................... 1855
Ault. Edwin D..................... 1868
Austin Fred. John................. 1862
Aylen John........................ 1857
Aylen James....................... 1863
Backhouse, John B................. 1870
Bain. D. S. E..................... 1868
Baird, James...................... 1870
Baker. Albert..................... 1848
Barclay, George................... 1870
*Barnston, James [ad eun.]........ 1856
Battersby. Charles................ 1861
Baynes. George Aylmer............. 1869
Beattie. David.................... 1862
Beaudet. Alfred................... 1865
Beaudry, Lewis H.................. 1871
Bell. John, M.A................... 1866
Bellew. Alfred.................... 1852

Bergeron. Joseph.................. 1870
Bergin. Darby..................... 1847
Bessey. William E................. 1863
Bender. Prosper................... 1865
Bibaud. Jean. G. J................ 1843
Blackader. Alex. D., B.A.......... 1871
Blacklock. John J................. 1851
Blanchet, J. B.................... 1863
Blair. Robt. C.................... 1865
Bligh, John W..................... 1865
Bogart. Irvine.................... 1859
Boulter. George Henry............. 1852
Boyer. Louis...................... 1842
*Boylan, Andrew A................. 1857
*Bowman, William Edward........... 1860
Bower. Silas J.................... 1865
Bradley, William.................. 1869
Brathwait, Francis H.............. 1863
Brandon John...................... 1867
Breslin. William Irwin............ 1847
Brigham. Josiah S................. 1848
Brissett, Henry R................. 1871
Bristol, Amos S................... 1850
Brodeur, Alphonse................. 1863
Brooks, Samuel T.................. 1851
Browne, Arthur A., B.A............ 1872
Browse, Jacob E................... 1861
Brouse. William H................. 1847
Brown, Peter E.................... 1863
Bruneau. Adolphe.................. 1853

*Bruneau, Oliver T. [Hon.]	1843	D'Avignon, Fred. E.	1871
Bruneau. Onesime	1851	*Dease, Peter Warren	1847
Bryson, William G	1867	DeBonald, W.S.	1862
Bucke Richard Maurice	1862	DeBoucherville. Charles B	1843
Bucke, Edward H.	1852	DeGrosbois. T. B	1868
Buckle, John M. C	1869	Demorest. Durham, G. G	1852
Buckley, William P.	1870	Desaulniers, Antoine A	1863
Bull, George Joseph	1869	DeCelles. Charles D	1841
Bullen. Charles F	1864	Dupuis. Joseph, G. P.	1856
Burgess. John A	1868	Dice, George	1864
Burch. Benjamin T	1865	*Dick, James R	1842
Burland, John H.	1863	Dickinson, James J.	1846
Burland, William B.	1872	*Dickinson, George.	1867
Burrows, Philip	1866	Dickson. William W	1863
Burnham. Robert Wilkins	1860	Digby, James Winnit	1866
Burns. Alfred J.	1854	Dodd. John	1843
Burritt. Horatio C	1863	Donnelly. Charles H	1866
Butler, George C	1865	*Dorion, Severe	1843
*Buxton. John N	1849	*Dorland. Enoch P	1850
Campbell, Donald Peter	1862	Dougan, William	1867
Campbell. Francis Wayland	1860	Douglas. James [Hon.]	1847
Campbell. Geo. W.. M.A. [ad eun]	1843	Drake. Joseph M	1861
Campbell. Samuel	1866	Dubuc. Charlemagne	1864
Campbell. John	1869	*Duckett, Stephen	1853
Carey. Augur D. L. [ad eun]	1864	Duckett. William A.	1859
Cassidy, David M	1867	Dufort. Thadee A	1865
Cassidy, John F	1865	Duhamel. Louis	1860
Carroll, Robert W. W	1859	Duncan. George	1866
Carson. Augustus	1843	Duncan, Gideon M	1871
Carter, Samuel A	1859	Duncan, James S	1858
Casgrain, Charles E	1851	Duncan. John	1871
Cattanach. Andrew J	1871	*Dunn, William Oscar	1843
Chagnon. Vinceslaus, G.B	1861	Dunsmore. John M	1870
*Challinor. Francis	1849	Easton. John	1852
Cherry. William	1869	Edwards, Eliphalet G	1855
*Chesley. George Ashbold	1862	Elkinton. Arthur G	1862
Chevalier, Gustave	1860	Emery, Gordon J	1857
Chipman. Clarence J. H., B.A	1868	Emery, Allard	1866
Christie. John B	1865	English. T. F	1858
Christie. Thomas	1848	Erskine, John	1860
Church. Charles Howard	1862	Ethier, Calixte	1867
Church, Clarence R	1867	Evans. Griffith	1864
Church. Coller M	1855	Falkner Alexander	1866
Church. Levi R	1857	Farewell, G. McGill	1872
Church. Mills Kemble	1864	Farewell, W. G	1868
Church. Peter H	1846	Faulkner. George W	1871
Clarke, Octavius H.E	1870	Fenwick, George Edgeworth	1847
Clarke. Wallace. B.A	1871	Fergusson, Alexander A	1864
Clark, Richard A	1870	Fergusson, Alexander A	1866
Clemesha. John Wordsworth	1867	Finlayson, John	1834
Clement. Victor A	1869	Finnie. John T	1869
Cluness. Daniel	1870	*Fisher. John	1848
Codd. Alfred	1865	Fitzgerald, James	1865
Collins. Charles W	1869	Fortin, Pierre	1845
Comeau. John B	1870	*Foster, Stephen Sewell	1846
Cooke, Charles H	1866	Fraleigh, William S	1869
Cooke, Herman L	1867	Fraser, William	1836
Cooke. Sidney P	1869	Fraser, William H	1867
Copeland. Wm. L	1872	Fraser. Donald M	1869
Corbett. Augustus M	1854	Fraser, Donald	1868
Corbett. William H	1854	Freeman. Charles M	1871
Corlis, Josiah	1869	Fuller, W	1866
Carson, John	1866	Fuller, Horace L	1870
*Cowley, Thomas Mc J	1870	Fulton, James H	1863
Cox. Frank	1869	Garvey, Joseph	1852
Craik, Robert	1854	Gardner, Matthew	1871
Cram, Daniel C	1872	Gardner, William	1867
*Crawford. James [ad eun]	1854	Gascoyne, George E	1861
Crichton, Stuart	1865	Gauvreau, Elzéar	1855
*Culver. Joseph R	1848	Gauvreau. Louis H	1836
*Cunynghame. W. C. Thurlow	1858	Gendron. Thomas	1866
Daly. Guy D. F	1868	Gernon, George W	1872
Dansereau, Charles	1842	Gibb, George D	1846
Dansereau, Charles	1869	Gibson, John B	1855
Dansereau, Pierre	1855	Gibson, Edward B	1864

Gillies, John	1867	Killery, St. John	1862
Gilmour, Angus	1868	King, William M. H	1859
*Giroux, Philippe	1859	King, Reginald A.D	1868
Girdwood, Gilbert P	1865	King, Richard A	1867
Glen, C. W. E.	1858	*Kirkpatrick, A.	1856
Godfrey, Robert	1845	Kittson, John G	1869
Godfrey, Abraham C	1865	Knowles, James A	1866
Goforth, Franklin	1863	Kollmyer, Alex. H	1856
Gordon, Robert	1868	Laberge, Ed	1856
Gordon, William Wallace	1863	*Lang, Thos. D	1869
Graham, Charles E.	1866	Langrell, Richard T	1865
Graham, Henry	1863	Larocque, A.B	1847
Grant, Donald J.	1863	Law, D. W. C	1868
Grant, James A.	1854	Lawrence, Henry G. H	1862
Grant, William	1867	Leavitt, Julius	1866
Grenier, L. P. A.	1863	Leclair, George	1851
Gunn, James	1861	Leclair, Napoleon	1861
Gustin, William Claude	1863	Lee, James C	1856
Hagarty, Dan. M. J.	1868	*Lee, John Rolph	1848
*Hall, Archibald [ad eun]	1843	Legault, Daniel	1868
Hall, James B.	1866	Lemoine, Charles	1850
Hall, J. W.	1848	Lepailleur, Leonard	1848
Halliday, James T.	1866	Leprohon, John L.	1843
Hamilton, Andrew W	1859	Lindsay, Heriot	1861
Hamilton, Charles S.	1868	Lister, James	1862
Hamilton, John R.	1871	Locke, C. T. A.	1872
Hamilton, Rufus Edward	1861	Logan, David D	1842
Hamel, Joseph Alexander	1856	Logie, William	1833
Hammond, James H	1869	*Long Alexander	1844
Harding, F. W.	1868	Longley, Edmund	1866
Harkin, Henry	1867	Longpre, Pierre F	1848
Harkin, William	1858	Loupret, Andre	1850
Harkness, John	1862	Loux, William	1870
Harkness, Andrew	1869	Loverin, Nelson	1855
Harrison, David Howard	1864	Lovett, William	1870
Hart, Frederick W.	1835	Lucas, T. D'Arcy	1869
Hays, James	1866	Lundy, Edward Lewis	1862
Hebert, P. Zotique	1872	Lyon, Arthur	1861
Henderson, Alexander A	1870	MacDonald, Angus	1863
*Henderson, Peter	1843	*MacDonald, Colin	1853
*Henry, Walter (Hon.)	1853	MacDonald, Roderick	1834
Henry, Walter J.	1856	MacIntosh, Robert	1863
Hervey, Jones J. G.	1866	Mack, Francis Lewis	1862
Hetherington, Harry	1872	Mackie, John R.	1865
Hickey, Charles E	1866	*Maclem, Samuel S	1859
Hingston, W. H.	1851	MacNabb, Francis A. L	1870
Holden, Rufus	1844	Madill, John	1867
Hollwell, John	1868	Major, George W.. B.A	1871
*Holmes, Andrew F. (ad eun)	1843	Malcolm, John Rolph	1861
Howard, James	1867	*Malhoit, Alfred	1846
Howard, Robert	1872	Malloch, Edward C	1863
Howard, R. Palmer	1848	Malloch, William B	1867
Howden, Robert	1857	Mallory, Albert S	1872
Howitt, William H	1870	Marcean, Louis T	1872
Howland, Francis D	1867	Markell, Richard	1867
Hulbert, Edward Augustus	1860	*Marr, Israel P	1849
Hulbert, George W	1859	Marr, Walker H	1859
Hunt, J. H., L.R.C.S.I	1869	Marston, Alonzo W	1871
Hunt, Lewis G	1871	Marston, John J	1863
Hurd, Edward P	1865	Mason, James Lindsay, M.A.	1863
Irvine, James C	1866	Mathieson, John H	1871
Ives, Eli	1863	Mathieson, Niel	1870
*Jackson, A. Thomas	1846	Mayrand, William	1847
Johnston, J. C	1867	McArthur, Robert D	1867
Johnston, Thomas G	1871	McCallum, Duncan C	1850
*Jones, Thomas W. (ad eun)	1854	McCarthy, William	1867
Jones, Jonathan C	1865	McConkey, J. C.	1872
Jones, W. Justus	1856	*McCord, John D	1864
Keefer, William N., B.A.	1869	McCrimmon, Donald A	1869
*Keefer, Thomas	1859	*McCulloch Michael (Hon.)	1843
Kelly, Clinton Wayne	1867	McCurdy, John	1866
*Kelly, William	1846	*MacDiarmid, John Duncan	1847
Kemp, William	1864	McDiarmid, Donald	1867
Kennedy, Richard A	1864	McDonnell, Angus	1852
*Kerr, James	1858	McDonnell, Æneas	1849

Name	Year	Name	Year
McDougall, Peter A.	1847	*Paterson, James	1855
McDougall, Peter A.	1864	Paterson, James	1864
McEwen, Findlay	1870	*Patee, George	1858
MacFarlane, William	1869	Pallen, Montrose A.	1864
Macfie, James	1869	Patton, Edward K.	1867
McGarry, James	1858	Pegg, Austin J.	1872
McGeachy, William	1867	Pegg, Charles H.	1867
McGill, William	1848	Perrault, Victor	1852
McGillivray, Donald	1861	Perrier, John	1868
McGowan, Henry W.	1867	Perrigo, James, M.A.	1870
McGrath, Thomas	1849	Phelan, Cornelius J. R.	1865
McGregor, Duncan	1861	*Phealan, Joseph P.	1854
McInnes, Walter J.	1865	Philip, David L.	1861
McIntosh, James	1859	Picault, A. C. E.	1857
McIntosh, Donald J	1870	Pickup, John Walworth	1860
McIntyre, Peter A.	1867	*Pinet, Alexis	1847
McKelcan, George Lloyd	1860	Pinet, Alex. R.	1864
McKay, John	1869	Poussette, Arthur Courthope	1860
McKay, Walter	1854	Powell, Israel Wood	1860
McLaren, Peter	1861	Powell, Newton W	1853
McLaren, Peter	1860	Powers, George W	1861
McLaren, Peter	1872	Powers, Lafontaine B	1864
McLean, Alexander	1860	Pringle, George	1855
McLean, Archibald	1867	Proudfoot, John S.	1868
McMicking, George	1851	Proudfoot, Alex.	1869
McMillan, John	1857	Proulx, Philias	1844
McMillan, Louis J. A.	1860	Provost, E. Gilbert	1859
McMurray, Samuel	1841	Quarry, James J.	1868
*McNaughton, E. P.	1849	Quesnel, Jules M.	1849
McNeece, James	1866	Rae, John Hamilton (Hon.)	1853
McTaggert, Alexander	1869	Rainville, Pierre	1853
McVean, John M	1865	Rambaut, John	1859
Menne, John, M.R.C.S.L	1869	Rattray, Charles J.	1871
Meigs, Malcolm R.	1865	Raymond, Oliver	1850
*Meredith, Thomas L. B.	1842	Read, Herbert H.	1861
Mignault, Henri Adolphe	1860	Rednor, Horace P.	1864
Miller, Robert	1870	Reddy, John (ad eun)	1856
Mitchell, Fred H	1871	Reed, Thomas D.	1871
Moffatt, John Edward	1862	Reid, Alex. Peter	1858
Moffatt, Walter	1868	Reid, John A.	1871
Mondelet, Wm. H.	1868	Reid, Kenneth	1864
Mongenais, Napoleon	1865	Reynolds, Robert T.	1836
Mount, John W	1855	*Reynolds, Thomas	1842
Moore, Joseph	1852	Richard, Marcel	1864
Moore, Richard	1853	Ridley, Henry Thomas	1852
Moore, Robert C.	1869	*Riel, Etienne R. R.	1857
*Morrin, Josh (Hon.)	1850	Rinfret, Ferdinand R.	1868
*Morrison, David R	1869	*Rintoul David M.	1854
Morrison, John, M.A.	1872	Richardson, John R.	1865
Munro, James T.	1872	Roberts, Edward T.	1859
*Nelson, Horace	1861	Roberts, John E., B. A.	1867
*Nelson, Wolfred (Hon.)	1848	Robertson, James	1865
Nelson, Wolfred D. E.	1872	Robertson, David	1864
Nicol, William R	1872	Robertson, David T.	1857
Nichols, Charles Richard	1862	Robertson, Patrick	1867
Nesbitt, James A.	1868	Robillard, Adolphe	1860
O'Brien, Thomas B.P.	1862	Robinson, Wesley	1872
O'Callaghan, Cornelius H	1854	Robitaille, Louis	1860
*O'Carr, Peter	1857	Robitaille, L. T.	1858
*O'Connor, Daniel A	1861	Roddick, Thomas G	1868
O'Dea, James Joseph	1859	Rodger, Thomas A.	1869
Odell, William	1849	Rooney, Robert F.	1870
O'Leary, James	1866	Ross, George, M.A.	1866
O'Leary, Patrick	1859	Ross, Thomas	1863
Oliver, James W	1867	Ross, Henry	1872
O'Reilly, Charles	1872	Ross, William G.	1871
Osler, Wm.	1872	Rugg, Henry C.	1865
Padfield, Chas. Wm.	1868	Rumsey, William	1859
Painchaud, Edward S. L	1848	Ruttan, Allan	1852
Palmer, Lorin L.	1867	*Sabourin, Moise	1849
Paquin, Jean M.	1843	Sampson, Jas. (Hon.)	1847
Paradis, Henry	1848	Sanderson, George W	1850
Paradis, Pierre E.	1867	Savage, Thomas Y.	1854
Parker, Rufus S.	1866	Savage, Alex. C.	1866
Parker, Charles S.	1866	Sawyer, James E	1863

Schmidt, Samuel B.	1847	Theriault, F. D.	1863
Scholfield, David T.	1869	Therien, Honore.	1864
Scott, Stephen A.	1855	*Thomson, James.	1842
Scott, W. E.	1844	Thompson, Robert	1852
*Scriven, George Augustus	1846	Trenholme, Edward Henry.	1862
Seager, Francis R.	1870	Trudel, Eugene.	1844
Seguin, Andre.	1848	Turgeon, Louis G.	1860
Senkler, A. E.	1863	Tuzo, Henry A.	1853
*Sewell, Stephen C. (ad eun)	1843	Ussher, Henry	1861
Sewell, Colin (ad eun).	1869	Vannerman, Jonathan A.	1850
Sharpe, Wm. James	1872	Vercoe. Henry L.	1865
Shaver, Peter Rolph	1854	Vicat, John R.	1867
Shaver, R. N.	1857	Wagner, A. Dixon.	1872
Shoebottom, Henry.	1857	Wagner, William H.	1844
*Simard, Amable.	1852	Wakeham, William.	1866
Simpson, Thomas	1854	Walker. Robert.	1851
Smallwood, John R.	1858	Walsh, Edmond C.	1866
*Smith, Daniel D.	1868	Wanless, John R.	1867
*Smith, Edward W.	1859	Warren, Frank	1872
Smith, Norman A	1870	Warren, Henry.	1860
Smyth, T. W.	1848	Waugh. William S.	1872
Sparham, Eric B.	1852	Webb, James T. S.	1871
Sparham, Terence.	1841	Weilbrenner, Remi Claude.	1851
*Squire, William Wood, M.A.	1864	Weir, Richard.	1852
Stanton. George	1868	Wherry, John.	1862
Starke. George A.	1872	Whitcomb, Josiah G.	1848
*Staunton. Andrew Aylmer	1845	Whitford, R.	1857
Stevens, Alex. D.	1857	Whitwell, William P. O.	1860
Stevenson. James McGregor	1856	Whyte, Joseph A.	1870
*Stevenson. John L.	1855	*Widmer, Christopher (Hon.)	1847
Stevenson. Robert A.	1871	Wilcox, Marshall B.	1868
Stewart, Alexander.	1872	Wilson, Benjamin S.	1856
Stewart, John Alexander.	1862	Wilson, Robert M.	1850
Stewart, James	1869	Wilson, William	1857
Stephenson. James.	1859	*Wilscam. John Wilbrod.	1846
Stimpson, Alfred O.	1868	Wolverton, Algeron, B.A.	1867
Shirk, George.	1865	Woods. David.	1869
Stowbridge, James Gordon.	1862	Wood, George C.	1849
Sutherland, Fred. Dunbar	1861	Wood. George.	1863
Sutherland, William.	1836	Wood. Hannibal W	1865
Sutherland. William	1870	Woodfull, Sam. Pratt.	1864
Switzer, John E. K.	1865	Workman, Benjamin	1853
Tabb, Silas, E., M.A.	1869	Workman, Joseph.	1835
Tait, Henry Thomas.	1860	Worthington, Edward (ad eun).	1868
Taylor, William H.	1844	Wright, Henry P.	1872
Taylor. Sullivan A	1870	Wright, Stephen	1859
Tew, Herbert S.	1864	Wright, William	1848
Temple, James A	1865	Wye, John A.	1868
Thayer, Linus O.	1859	Youker, William.	1870

MASTERS OF ARTS.

Bancroft, Rev. Charles (ad eun)	1855	Gibb, George D., M.D. (Hon.)	1856
Bancroft, Rev. C., B.A., Junior.	1870	Gibson, Thomas A. (Hon.)	1856
Baynes, Donald, B.A.	1867	Gilman, Francis E., B.A.	1865
Bethune. Meredith Blenkarne, B.A.	1869	Gould, Edwin, B.A.	1860
*Bothwell, John A., B.A.	1868	Graham, John H. (Hon.)	1859
Bowman. Wm. M. (Hon.)	1859	Green, Joseph, B.A.	1864
Boyd, John, B.A.	1864	Hall, William, B.A.	1867
Browne. Dunbar, B.A., B.C.L.	1861	Hart, Lewis A.. B.A.	1869
Butler, Rev. John (Hon.).	1852	Hicks, Francis W., B.A.	1870
Carmichael, Rev. J., B.A.	1871	Howe, Henry Aspinwall (Hon.)	1855
Chamberlin. Brown, D.C.L. (ad eun)	1857	Kähler, Frederick A.. B.A.	1872
Chapman. Rev. Charles, M.A., London Univ. (ad eun.)	1872	Kemp, Rev. Alexander F. (Hon.)..	1863
Clarke, Wallace. B.A., M.D.	1872	Kennedy, George T., B.A.	1872
Cornish, Rev. George. B.A.	1860	Kennedy, Rev. John, B.A.	1860
Cushing, Lemuel, B.A., B.C.L.	1867	Kirby, James, B.A., B.C.L.	1862
Davidson, Rev. Jas. B.A.	1866	*Leach, Robert A., B.A., B.C.L.	1860
Davidson, Charles P.. B.A., B.C.L.	1867	McCord, David R., B.A., B.C.L.	1867
Davidson. Leonidas H., B.A.	1867	McGregor, James, B.A.	1868
DeWitt, Caleb S., B.A.	1864	McLaren, John R., B.A.	1868
Dougall, John R.. B.A	1867	Markgraf, Charles F. A. (Hon.).	1865
Duff, Archibald, B.A.	1867	Mason, James L., B.A.	1863
		Mattice, Corydon J., B.A.	1862

Morris, Alex. B.A., B.C.L.	1852	Ross, George, B.A., M.D.	1866
Morrison, Rev. James D., B.A.	1868	Stewart. Rev. Colin Campbell, B.A.	1870
Morrison, John, B.A.	1870	Tabb, Silas Everett, B.A.	1869
Perkins, John A., B.A.	1862	Trenholme, Norman W.. B.A.,B.C.L	1867
Perrigo, James, B.A.	1869	Wicksteed, Richard G., B.A., B.C.L.	1866
*Plimsoll, Reginald J., B.A.	1862	Wilkie, Daniel (Hon.)	1866
Ramsay, Robert, A., B.A., B.C.L.	1867	Wilson, John, B.A.	1870
Robins, Sampson Paul, B.A.	1868	Wotherspoon, Ivan Tolkien, B.A.	1869
Rodger, David (Hon.)	1857		

BACHELORS OF CIVIL LAW.

Abbott, Christopher C.	1850	Farmer, William O.	1866
Abbott, John J. C.	1854	Fisher, Roswell C.	1869
Adams, Abel.	1867	Fisk, John J.	1868
Allan, Irvine.	1862	Foran, Thomas P.	1870
Archibald, John Sprott, B.A.	1870	Franks, Albert W.	1871
Archambeault, Joseph L. C.	1871	Gairdiner, William F.	1856
Armstrong, Louis.	1861	Galarneau, Joseph Antoine	1864
Ascher, Isidore G.	1863	Gauthier Zephirin.	1859
Aylen, John, M.D.	1861	Geoffrion, Christopher A.	1866
Aylen, Peter, B.A.	1854	Gibb, James R.	1868
*Badgley, Frank H.	1852	Gilman, Francis E., M. A.	1865
Bagg, Robert Stanley.	1871	Girouard, Desire.	1860
Barnston, John G.	1856	Gordon, Asa.	1867
Barry, Denis.	1872	Grenier, Amedé L. W.	1863
Baynes, Edward Alfred	1867	Hall, William A.	1863
Benjamin, Lewis N.	1865	Harnett, Wm. de Courcy.	1870
Bethune, Meredith B., M.A.	1869	Hart, Lewis A., M.A.	1869
*Bothwell, John A.	1866	Hemming, Edward J.	1855
Bouthillier, Charles F.	1867	Holton, Edward.	1865
Boyd, John, B.A.	1864	Houghton, John G. K.	1863
Blanchard, Athanase.	1862	Howard, Rice M.	1869
Browne, Dunbar, M.A.	1858	Howlisten, Alexander.	1865
Bullock, William E., B.A.	1863	Jodoin, Isaie.	1858
Butler, Thomas L.	1865	Johnston, Edwin R.	1866
Calder, John.	1871	Jones, Richard A. A.	1854
Carden, Henry.	1860	Joseph, Joseph O.	1864
Caron, Adolph P.	1865	Keller, Francis J.	1869
Carter, Christopher B.	1866	Kelley, John P.	1862
Carter, Edward (Hon.).	1864	Kemp, Edson, B.A.	1860
Chamberlin, Brown.	1850	Kenny, William R.	1865
Chamberlin, John, Junr.	1867	Kirby, James, M.A.	1862
Charland, Alfred.	1863	Kitson, George R. W.	1867
Chauveau, Alexandre.	1867	Lacoste, Arthur.	1869
Cocquet, Ambroise.	1865	Laflamme, R. G (Hon.).	1856
Conroy, Robert Hughes.	1865	Laflamme, Leopold.	1869
Cowan, Robert C.	1862	Lafrenaye, P. R. (Hon.).	1856
Cruikshank, William.	1872	Lambe, William B.	1850
Curran, Joseph C.	1862	Lanctot, Mederic.	1860
Cushing, Charles.	1869	Larose, Telesphore.	1860
Cushing, Lemuel, Junr., M.A.	1865	Laurier, Wilfred.	1864
Daly, J. G.	1858	Lay, Warren Amos.	1867
Dansereau, Arthur	1865	Lawlor, Richard S.	1865
Darby, Daniel.	1870	Leach, David S.	1861
Darey, Pierre J., M.A	1868	*Leach, Robert A., M.A.	1860
David, Alphonse.	1872	Lefebvre, Frederick.	1863
Davidson, Charles P., M.A.	1863	Lonergan, Michael L. S.	1871
Davidson, Leonidas Heber, M.A.	1863	Loranger, Louis George.	1863
Day, Edmund T.	1864	Lyman, Elisha Stiles.	1865
Desaulniers, Henri Lesieur.	1864	Lyman, Frederick S., B.A.	1869
Desrochers, Jean L. B.	1861	Lynch, Wm. W.	1868
Doak, George O.	1863	Mackenzie, Frederick.	1861
Doherty, Thomas J.	1868	Major, Edward James.	1871
Dorion, Adelard A. P.	1862	Marler, William DeM., B.A.	1872
Doutre, Pierre.	1858	McCord, David Ross, M.A.	1867
Doutre, Gonzalvo.	1861	McCormack, David.	1872
Driscoll, Netterville H.	1861	*McGee, Thomas D'Arcy.	1861
Drummond, William D.	1867	McIntosh, John, B.A.	1868
Dubuc, Joseph.	1869	McLaren, John J.	1868
Duchesnay, Henri J. T.	1866	McLaren, John Robert, M.A.	1860
Dunlop, John.	1860	McLaurin, John Rice.	1867
Duprat, Pierre N.	1866	McMaster, Donald.	1871
Durand, Naphtalie	1864	Merry, John Wesley	1870

Messier, Joseph S. 1868
Mitchell, Albert Edward 1867
Molson. Alexander 1851
Monk, Ed. Cornwallis 1870
Morris, Alexander, M.A. 1850
Morris, John L. 1860
Nagle, Sarsfield B. 1862
Nutting, Charles A. 1872
Ouimet. Adolphe P. 1861
Papineau, Joseph G. 1869
Piche. Aristide 1868
Perry, Joseph 1869
Pariseault, Chas. Ambroise 1859
Perkins, John A., M.A. 1860
*Plimsoll, Reginald J., M.A 1861
Power. Alexander W. A 1868
Ramsay, Robert A. M. A 1866
Richard, Damase F.S. 1859
Richard, Emery Edward. 1867
Richard. Edward E. 1868
Rixford, Emmet Hawkins. 1865
Robidoux. Emery 1866
Rochon. Charles A. 1861
Rose, William 1866
Sabourin, Ernest 1863
Sarrasin. Ferdinand Leon 1871
Sexton, James Ponsonby 1860

Short, Robert 1867
Sicotte, Victor B. 1862
Snowdon, H. L. 1856
Stephens, George W 1863
Stephens, Romeo H 1850
Stephens. Chas. O. 1864
Tait. Melbourne. 1862
Taschereau. Arthur 1864
Taylor, Reid. 1869
Terril, Joseph Lee 1865
Torrance. Fred. W.. M.A .. (Hon.) . 1856
Trenholme, Edward H., M.D 1865
Trenholme. Norman W. M.A 1865
Vandall, Phillipe. 1865
Vilbon, Chas. A 1863
Walsh, Thomas Joseph 1863
Watts, William J., B.A 1869
Welch, Alfred 1864
Wicksteed, Richard G., M.A. 1864
Wight, James H. 1868
Wood. Franc Ogilvie. 1870
Wotherspoon, Ivan T., (Laval), [ad
      eun]. 1869
Wright, William Mackay, B.A 1863
Wurtele. Charles J. C 1863
Wurtele, Jonathan S. C. (Hon.). ... 1870

Bachelors of Arts.

Allworth, John. 1872
Anderson, Jacob de Witt. 1866
Archibald, John Sprott. 1867
Aylen. Peter 1850
Bancroft. Rev. Chas., Junior 1866
Barnston. Alexander 1857
Baynes. Donald 1864
Beckett, William Henry. 1866
Bethune. Meredith Blenkarne 1866
Blackader, Alex. D 1870
Bockus, Charles E. 1852
*Bothwell. John A 1864
Boyd, John 1861
Brewster. William 1865
Brooks, Charles H. 1868
Browne, Arthur Adderley 1866
Browne, Dunbar 1856
Browne, Thomas 1853
Bullock, William E. 1860
Cameron, James 1871
Carmichael, James. 1867
Cassels, Robert, (Morrin). 1866
Chipman, Clarence 1866
Christie, John H. 1872
Clarke, Wallace. 1869
Cline, John D. 1871
Cook, Archibald H. (Morrin). 1869
Clowe, John D. 1863
Cornish, Rev. Geo., B.A., London
      Univ. (ad eun.). 1856
Crothers, W. J. 1872
Coussirat. Rev. Adrian D. (ad. eun). 1871
Cushing. Lemuel. 1863
Dart, William J. 1868
Davidson, Charles Peers. 1863
Davidson, Rev. Jas. (ad eun) 1863
Davidson. Leonidas Heber 1863
Dey. William J. 1871
DeWitt, Caleb S. 1861
Dougall, Duncan 1860
Dougall, John Redpath. 1860
Drummond. Chas. G. B 1862
Duff, Archibald.. 1864
Duncan, Alexander 1867

Ells. Robert 1872
Fairbairn, Thomas. 1863
Ferguson. John S. 1861
*Ferrier, Robert W 1857
Fessenden. Elisha Joseph.. 1863
Fortin. Rev. Octave (ad eun) 1867
Fowler, William 1865
Fowler, Elbert 1865
Fraser. John (Morrin). 1869
Gibb, Charles 1865
Gilman. Francis Edward. 1862
Gore, Frederick. 1861
Gould, Edwin 1856
Grandy, John. 1866
Greenshields, Edward. 1869
Green, Joseph. 1861
Green, Lonsdale. 1864
Hall, William 1861
Hart, Lewis A. 1866
Harrington, Bernard I 1869
Hicks, Francis W 1864
Hindley. John. 1868
Hodge, D. W. K. 1872
Holiday, Caleb S. 1870
Jones, Montgomery. 1869
Johnston, James A. 1870
Joseph. Montefiore 1870
Kähler, Frederick A. 1869
Kelley, Frederick W 1871
Kemp, Edson 1859
Kennedy, George T. 1868
*Kershaw, Philip G 1867
Kirby, James. 1859
Krans, Edward H 1865
Laing, Robert. 1868
*Leach, Robert A 1857
Lewis, Albert R. 1869
Lyman, Frederick Stiles. 1863
Major, George W. 1870
Marler, Wm. DeM. 1868
Mason. James L. 1859
Mattice, Corydon J 1859
Maxwell, John 1872
McCord, D. Ross. 1863

McDuff. Alexander Ramsay	1866	Petit, Rev. Charles B	1850
McGregor, James	1864	Phillips, Charles W	1852
McGregor, Duncan	1871	*Plimsoll, Reginald J	1858
McIntosh, John	1870	Ramsay, Robert Anstruther	1862
McKenzie, John (Morrin)	1867	Redpath, Geo. D	1857
McKenzie, Robert	1869	Robertson, Alex	1870
McLaren, John R	1856	Robins, Sampson Paul	1863
McLaren, Harry	1858	Ross, George	1862
McLean, Neil W. (Morrin)	1866	Russell, Henry (Morrin)	1869
McLennan, Duncan H	1871	Scott, Henry C. (Morrin)	1866
McLeod, Hugh	1866	Sherrill, Alvan F	1864
McLeod, Finlay C	1872	Slack, George	1868
McOuat, Walter	1865	Stothem, George T	1852
Merritt. David Prescott	1863	Stewart, Colin Campbell	1867
Moore, Francis X	1868	Tabb, Silas Everett	1866
Morris, William	1859	Torrance, Edward	1871
Morris, Alexander	1849	Torrance, John Fraser	1872
Morrison, John	1866	Trenholme, Norman Wm	1863
Morrison, James D	1865	Tupper, James S	1871
Morrison, David E	1870	Walker, Thomas	1860
Muir. John N	1864	Wallace, Robert W	1872
*Muir, Rev. E. P. (ad eun)	1865	Watts, Wm. John	1866
Munro, Gustavus	1871	Whillans, Robert	1872
Munro, Murdoch	1872	Wicksteed, Richard G	1863
Naylor, W. H	1872	Wilson, John	1866
Oliver. Theophilus H. (Morrin)	1866	Wood, Franc O	1869
Pease. George H	1864	Wood, Thomas F	1869
Perrigo, James	1866	Wotherspoon, Ivan T. (Morrin)	1866
Perkins, John A	1858	Wright, William McKay	1861

Graduates in Civil Engineering.

Barnston, Alexander, B.A	1859	Gould, James H	1872
Bell, Robert	1861	Kirby, Charles H	1860
Crawford. Robert	1859	McLennan, Christopher	1859
Doupe. Joseph	1861	Reid, John Lestock	1863
Edwards, George	1863	Rixford, Gulian Pickering	1864
Frost, George H	1860	Ross, Arthur	1860
Gaviller, Maurice	1863	Savage, Joseph	1860
Gooding, Oliver	1868	Walker, Thomas, B.A	1860

* Deceased.